Nine Patch & Snowball Quilts

by Elsie Campbell

Chitra Publications

www.QuiltTownUSA.com

Chitra Publications
2 Public Avenue
Montrose, Pennsylvania 18801-1220

First Printing 2003

Library of Congress Cataloging-in-Publication Data

Campbell, Elsie, 1949-
   Nine Patch & Snowball quilts/ by Elsie Campbell.
      p. cm.
   ISBN 1-885588-53-4
   1. Patchwork—Patterns. 2. Quilting—Patterns. I. Title:
Nine Patch and Snowball quilts. II. Title.
   TT835.C3565 2003
   746.46'041—dc21

              2003008034

Edited by: Debra Feece
Design and Illustrations: Brenda Pytlik
Photography: Van Zandbergen Photography, Brackney, Pennsylvania

Our Mission Statement:

*We publish quality quilting magazines and books
that recognize, promote, and inspire self-expression.
We are dedicated to serving our customers
with respect, kindness, and efficiency.*

www.QuiltTownUSA.com

Dedication

This book is dedicated to the memory of my mother, Ella May Goebel Reusser, who was my favorite quilting partner—and biggest fan.

Introduction

Dear Friends,

Several years ago, I received an assignment from Chitra Publications to write a Design Challenge for *Traditional Quiltworks* magazine. The topic was to be a combination of two simple quilt blocks, the Nine Patch and Snowball. I wondered how something as simple as these blocks could become anything as exciting and different as past design challenges. Then I started asking myself Sharyn Craig's favorite question, "What If...?" and the designs started flowing.

Are these blocks easy to piece? Yes! Even most beginning quilters have the skills to stitch these uncomplicated blocks. Then what is the big deal? The big deal is the fact that there are so many creative ways to manipulate color and value to achieve complicated-looking quilts. After playing with these blocks on graph paper, I was amazed at the variety of patterns that emerged.

I truly enjoyed this challenge, so I enlisted the help of some of my friends in Miss Kitty's Quilters of Dodge City, Kansas, to make my drawings become actual quilts. We had several pleasant days working together on the projects you'll find in this book. I hope you'll enjoy making and using your versions of these Nine Patch and Snowball quilts as much as I have.

"Piece-fully,"

Elsie

Acknowledgements

Thanks to these members of Miss Kitty's Quilter's Guild of Dodge City, Kansas, for their help and encouragement in completing the projects for this book: Joan Becker, Doris Callaway, Louise Feldt, Rosella Hennessey, Vera Kenton, Pat Rebein, Cricket Turley, Berenice Wagner, Rose Warner, and Doll Yunker. A very special 'thank you' goes to my patient and supportive husband Ken Campbell for all the meals he prepared while this book was in progress and for adding his computer savvy to my quilting knowledge while I wrote this text.

Contents

Hearts of Gold

*I purposely sized this quilt to fit a child's twin bed. Wouldn't **"Hearts of Gold"** be perfect for a girl's bedroom? Add the matching pillow (shown on page 6) or pillow sham with a dust ruffle, and won't she be pleased? Or, instead of hearts, appliqué stars to suit the youngest man in your household. (A suitable star pattern is provided on the inside back cover.)*

Quilt Size: 53 1/2" x 77 1/2"
Block Size: 6" square

Materials

- 1 3/4 yards off-white print
- 1 yard gold print
- 1 yard medium blue print
- 5 1/2 yards dark blue print
- Paper-backed fusible web (optional)
- 4 1/2 yards backing fabric
- 58" x 82" piece of batting

Cutting

The appliqué heart pattern (on page 27) is full size and does not include a seam allowance. All other dimensions include a 1/4" seam allowance. Make a template for the heart pattern. Trace around the template on the right side of the fabric and add a 1/8" to 3/16" turn-under allowance when cutting the fabric pieces out. Cut the lengthwise strips before cutting other pieces from the same yardage.

For the Snowball blocks:
- Cut 38: 6 1/2" squares, off-white print
- Cut 152: 2 1/2" squares, medium blue print
- Cut 38: hearts, gold print NOTE: *If you choose to use paper-backed fusible web, apply it to the fabric before cutting the hearts. See the* General Directions *for instructions and adhere it according to the manufacturer's instructions.*

For the Nine Patch blocks:
- Cut 3: 2 1/2" x 44" strips, off-white print
- Cut 11: 2 1/2" x 44" strips, medium blue print
- Cut 10: 2 1/2" x 44" strips, dark blue print

Also:
- Cut 8: 3/4" x 44" strips, gold print, for the middle border

- Cut 2: 1" x 45" lengthwise strips, dark blue print, for the inner border
- Cut 2: 1" x 70" lengthwise strips, dark blue print, for the inner border
- Cut 2: 5 1/2" x 56" lengthwise strips, dark blue print, for the outer border
- Cut 2: 5 1/2" x 70" lengthwise strips, dark blue print, for the outer border
- Cut 4: 2 1/2" x 72" lengthwise strips, dark blue print, for the binding

Directions

For the Snowball blocks:

1. Referring to the *General Directions* for Snowball construction (page 31), stitch a Snowball block using a 6 1/2" off-white print square and four 2 1/2" medium blue print squares, as shown.

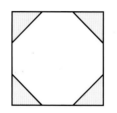

2. To find the center, fold a Snowball block in half and crease. Using the crease for alignment, appliqué a heart to a Snowball block to make a Heart of Gold block. Make 38. Set them aside.

For the Nine Patch blocks:

1. Referring to the *General Directions* for Nine Patch blocks, Method #1, (page 31) stitch a pieced panel from two 2 1/2" x 44" dark blue print strips and one medium blue print strip, as shown.

Make 5. Press the seams toward the dark blue print. Cut seventy-eight 2 1/2" slices from the panels and set them aside.

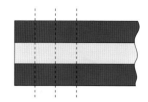

2. In the same manner, stitch 3 pieced panels from the remaining 2 1/2" x 44" medium blue print strips and the 2 1/2" x 44" off-white print strips, as shown. Cut thirty-nine 2 1/2" slices from the panels.

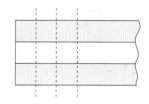

3. Lay out 2 dark blue/medium blue slices and one medium blue/off-white slice. Stitch them into a Nine Patch, as shown. Make 39.

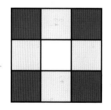

Assembly

1. Lay out the Hearts of Gold and Nine Patch blocks alternately in 11 rows of 7. Stitch the blocks into rows and join the rows.

2. Measure the length of the quilt. Trim the 1" x 70" dark blue print strips to that measurement and stitch them to the sides of the quilt.

3. Measure the width of the quilt, including the borders. Trim the 1" x 45" dark blue print strips to that measure-

(Continued on page 27)

Hearts of Gold Pillow

Make this pillow to coordinate with the **"Hearts of Gold"** *quilt on page 4. I love making miniature quilts, but I don't have wall space to display a lot of them, so I decided that a pillow is the perfect solution. If you'd prefer, you can finish this piece as a miniature quilt for a child's favorite doll.*

Pillow Size: 16" square
Block Size: 3" square

Materials

- 1/4 yard off-white print
- 1/8 yard gold print
- 1/4 yard medium blue print
- 1 yard dark blue print
- 18" square of muslin
- Paper-backed fusible web (optional)
- 2 yards 1/4" diameter cotton cording
- 18" square of batting
- 16" square pillow form

Cutting

The small heart appliqué pattern (on page 27) is full size and does not include a seam allowance. Make a template for the heart pattern. Trace around the template on the right side of the fabric and add a 1/8" to 3/16" turn-under allowance when cutting the fabric pieces out. All other dimensions include a 1/4" seam allowance.

For the Snowball blocks:

- Cut 9: 3 1/2" squares, off-white print
- Cut 36: 1 1/2" squares, medium blue print
- Cut 9: small hearts, gold print
NOTE: *If you choose to use paper-backed fusible web, apply it to the fabric before cutting the hearts. See the* General Directions *for instructions and adhere it according to the manufacturer's instructions.*

For the Nine Patch blocks:

- Cut 1: 1 1/2" x 25" strip, off-white print
- Cut 4: 1 1/2" x 25" strips, medium blue print
- Cut 4: 1 1/2" x 25" strips, dark blue print

Also:

- Cut 4: 5/8" x 16" strips, gold print, for the middle border
- Cut 4: 3/4" x 15" strips, dark blue print, for the inner border
- Cut 4: 1 3/4" x 18" strips, dark blue print, for the outer border
- Cut 2: 12" x 16" rectangles, dark blue print, for the pillow back
- Cut 2: 2" x 38" bias strips, dark blue print, for the piping
- Cut 1: 18" square, muslin

Directions

For the Snowball blocks:

1. Referring to the *General Directions* for Snowball construction (page 31), stitch a Snowball block using a 3 1/2" off-white print square and four 1 1/2" medium blue print squares, as shown.

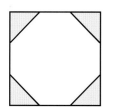

2. To find the center, fold a Snowball block in half diagonally and crease. Using the crease for alignment, appliqué a small heart to a Snowball block to make a Heart of Gold block. Make 9. Set them aside.

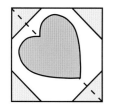

For the Nine Patch blocks:

1. Referring to the *General Directions* for Nine Patch blocks, Method #1, stitch a pieced panel from two 1 1/2" x 25" dark blue print strips and one medium blue print strip, as shown. Make 2. Press the seams toward the dark blue print. Cut thirty-two 1 1/2" slices from the panels and set them aside.

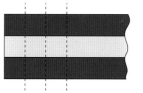

2. In the same manner, stitch a pieced panel from the remaining 1 1/2" x 25" medium blue print strips and the 1 1/2" x 25" off-white print strip, as shown. Cut sixteen 1 1/2" slices from the panel.

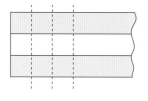

3. Lay out 2 dark blue/medium blue slices and one medium blue/off-white slice. Stitch them into a Nine Patch, as shown. Make 16.

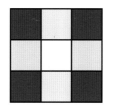

Assembly

1. Lay out the Hearts of Gold and Nine Patch blocks. Stitch the blocks into diagonal rows and join the rows.

2. With a rotary cutter and square ruler, square the pillow top to 13 1/4".

3. Trim two of the 3/4" x 15" dark blue print strips to 13 1/4" and stitch them to opposite sides of the pillow top.

4. Trim the remaining 3/4" x 15" dark blue print strips to 13 3/4" and stitch them to the top and bottom of the pillow top.

5. Measure the length of the pillow top. Trim 2 of the 5/8" x 16" gold print strips to that measurement and stitch them to opposite sides of the pillow top.

6. Measure the width of the pillow top, including the borders. Trim the remaining 5/8" x 16" gold print strips to that measurement and stitch them to the top and bottom of the pillow top.

7. In the same manner, trim 2 of the 1 3/4" x 18" dark blue print strips to fit the pillow top's length and stitch them to the sides of the pillow top.

8. Trim the remaining 1 3/4" x 18" dark blue print strips to fit the top and bottom of the pillow top.

9. Sandwich the 18" muslin square, batting, and pillow top. Quilt as desired.

10. Stitch the 2" x 38" dark blue bias strips together, end to end, to make a pieced strip.

11. Install the zipper foot on your sewing machine. Fold the pieced strip in half lengthwise, right side out, around the 1/4" diameter cotton cording and stitch next to the cording, as shown.

12. Baste the prepared piping along the outer edge on the right side of the pillow top, as shown. Note that the corners are slightly rounded. Set it aside.

13. Turn under 1/4" along one 16" edge of each 12" x 16" dark blue rectangle and edge stitch.

14. Fold the stitched edge of the dark blue rectangles under 2 1/2" and press.

15. Lay the dark blue rectangles right side down on the right side of the pillow top, overlapping the folded edges. Pin them in place.

16. Stitching from the pillow top side, stitch exactly on top of the basting stitches holding the piping in place, around the entire pillow, as shown.

17. Turn the pillow right side out through the opening created by the overlapped edges. NOTE: *There is no need to trim the corners. The extra fabric will pad the corners.*

18. Insert a 16" pillow form through the opening and enjoy your pillow!

Country Stars

When my friend Cricket Turley offered to help me finish some projects for this book, I was thrilled! I had an idea for a quilt, but didn't have time to make it, so Cricket chose a very traditional color scheme and stitched "Country Stars". It was her first attempt at piecing and quilting an entire bed-sized quilt. What a beautiful result!

Quilt Size: 70" x 94"
Block Size: 6" square

Materials

- 16 fat quarters (18" x 22") assorted white and off-white prints for the Snowballs
- 2 3/4 yards dark blue print for the Snowball blocks, outer border and binding
- 2 1/2 yards light red print
- Assorted blue prints to total 1 1/2 yards
- Assorted red prints to total 2 1/4 yards
- 5/8 yard tone-on-tone off-white print for the inner border
- 1/2 yard dark red print for the middle border
- 5 5/8 yards backing fabric
- 74" x 98" piece of batting

Cutting

All dimensions include a 1/4" seam allowance. Cut the lengthwise strips before cutting other pieces from the same yardage.

For the Snowball blocks:

- Cut 58: 6 1/2" squares, assorted white and off-white prints
- Cut 116: 2 1/2" squares, light red print
- Cut 116: 2 1/2" squares, dark blue print

For the Nine Patch blocks:

- Cut 90: 2 1/2 squares, assorted blue prints
- Cut 120: 2 1/2 squares, assorted white and off-white prints
- Cut 164: 2 1/2" squares, light red print
- Cut 157: 2 1/2" squares, assorted red prints

For the Border units:

- Cut 24: 2 1/2" x 6 1/2" strips, assorted white and off-white prints
- Cut 20: 2 1/2" x 4 1/2" rectangles, assorted white and off-white prints
- Cut 28: 2 1/2" squares, dark blue print

- Cut 20: 2 1/2" squares, light red print
- Cut 20: 2 1/2" squares, assorted red prints

Also:

- Cut 4: 2 1/2" squares assorted white and off-white prints, for the quilt corners
- Cut 8: 2" x 44" strips tone-on-tone off-white print, for the inner border
- Cut 8: 1 1/4" x 44" strips dark red print, for the middle border
- Cut 4: 4 1/4" x 88" lengthwise strips dark blue print, for the outer border
- Cut 4: 2 1/2" x 96" lengthwise strips dark blue print, for the binding

Directions

For the Snowball blocks:

1. Referring to the *General Directions* for Snowball construction (page 31), stitch a Snowball block using a 6 1/2" white or off-white print square, two 2 1/2" light red prints squares and two 2 1/2" dark blue print squares for the corners, as shown. Make 58. Set them aside.

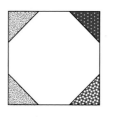

2. Referring to the *General Directions* for Nine Patch blocks, Method #2, stitch a Nine Patch block, using five 2 1/2" assorted blue print squares and four 2 1/2" assorted white and off-white print squares, as shown. Make 18. Set them aside.

3. In the same manner, stitch a Nine Patch block, using five 2 1/2" assorted red print squares and four 2 1/2" light red print squares, as shown. Make 17. Set them aside.

4. Stitch a Nine Patch block, as before, using three 2 1/2" assorted red print squares, two 2 1/2" assorted white and off-white print squares, and four 2 1/2" light red print squares, as shown. Make 24. Set them aside.

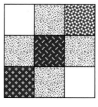

For the Border units:

1. Draw a diagonal line from corner to corner on the wrong side of each of two 2 1/2" dark blue print squares.

2. Lay a marked 2 1/2" dark blue print square on one end of a 2 1/2" x 6 1/2" white or off-white print strip. Stitch on the marked line. Press the square toward the corner of the strip, aligning the edges. Trim the seam 1/4" away from the stitching line. NOTE: *This is similar to the way you've stitched the Snowball corners.*

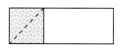

3. In the same manner, stitch the second marked dark blue print square to the opposite end of the white print strip, to make an "E" Border unit. Make 14. Set them aside. NOTE: *Pay careful attention to the orientation of the stitching*

(Continued on page 30)

Internet

Optical illusions have always fascinated me. When beautiful hand-dyed fabrics became available in gradated shades, the possibilities for making illusions in quilts was limited only by the quilter's imagination. I loved creating the effect of interwoven threads in **"Internet"** *and decided it reminded me of how intertwined our modern lives have become with the advent of the World Wide Web.*

Quilt Size: 56" x 68"
Block Size: 6" square

Materials

- 6 shades of each of 12 colors of hand-dyed solids, for a total of 72 colors. Number the fabrics in each color group from #1 to #6 with #1 being the lightest. You will need a fat eighth (11" x 18") of each color #1, 2, 3, 5, and 6, and a fat quarter (18" x 22") of each #4 fabric.
- 2 1/2 yards black solid
- 4 1/4 yards backing fabric
- 60" x 72" piece of batting

Cutting

Patterns A and B (page 29) are full size and include a 1/4" seam allowance, as do all dimensions given. Cut lengthwise strips before cutting other pieces from the same yardage.

From the hand-dyed fabrics:

- Cut 4: A's from the #4 fabric in each of 11 groups, for a total of 44 A's.
- Cut 5: A's from the remaining #4 fabric
- Cut 2: 1 1/2" x 13" strips each, from the remaining shades of hand-dyed solid

NOTE: *Set aside the leftover hand-dyed fabrics. You will need some of them again later.*

From the black:

- Cut 160: B's
- Cut 160: 2 1/2" squares
- Cut 4: 3 1/2" x 68" lengthwise strips, for the borders
- Cut 4: 2 1/2" x 72" lengthwise strips, for the binding

Directions

For the curved Snowball blocks:

1. On the work surface or design wall, lay out the A's in a pleasing color arrangement. Refer to the quilt photo and Assembly Diagram (page 28) as needed.

2. For the top, sides, and bottom edges, make partial Snowball blocks, as shown, stitching black solid B's to only

2 sides of the A's. Make 18. Place them back in the layout.

3. Stitch a black solid B in each corner of the remaining A's. Make 31.

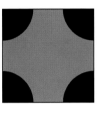

For the Nine Patch blocks:

1. Stitch three 1 1/2" x 13" strips from one color group together, gradating from #1 to #3. Make 2 of each color group for a total of 24 panels.

2. Cut four 2 1/2" sections from each panel. Set them aside.

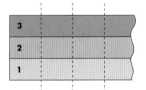

3. Stitch a #5 and a #6 strip from one color group together to make a panel. Make 2 of each color group for a total of 24 panels.

4. Cut four 2 1/2" sections from each panel of the colors used for the 4 A's and 5 from each panel of the color used for the 5 A's.

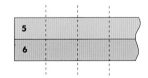

5. Starting in the upper left corner of the layout (refer to the Assembly Diagram on page 28), place 2 light sections, 2 dark sections, and four 2 1/2" black squares adjacent to the first 2 partial Snowball blocks. The light and dark sections should match the color

groups in the Snowball blocks. Place the #1 fabrics together in the center of the Nine Patch block and the #6 fabrics toward the center, as shown. Stitch the units together to make a Nine Patch block.

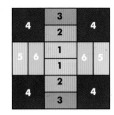

6. Place the block back in the layout and continue in the same manner to make a total of 32 Nine Patch blocks.

7. For the sides of the quilt, stitch partial Nine Patch blocks, as shown, matching the adjacent Snowball blocks. Make 8.

8. For the top and bottom of the quilt, lay out two 2 1/2" black squares, a light section, and 2 dark sections, matching the adjacent Snowball blocks. Cut a 1 1/2" x 2 1/2" #1 rectangle to match the #1 rectangle of the light section. Stitch the units together to make a partial Nine Patch block, as shown. Make 6.

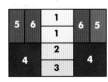

9. For the corners, lay out a 2 1/2" black square, a dark section, and a light section. Cut a 1 1/2" x 2 1/2" #1 rectangle to match the #1 rectangle of the light section. Stitch the units together to make a corner block. Make 4.

(Continued on page 28)

Baubles and Beads

Pat Rebein, Vera Kenton, and Doris Callaway, members of Miss Kitty's Quilter's Guild of Dodge City, Kansas, worked together to stitch Elsie Campbell's original design **"Baubles and Beads".** *Pinks and blues form the diagonal strings of beads. Machine quilted by Shelly Carmichael of Larned, Kansas.*

Quilt Size: 75 1/2" x 90 1/2"
Block Size: 7 1/2" square

Materials
- 3/4 yard pink print
- Assorted blue prints totaling 1 1/2 yards
- 1/2 yard turquoise print
- 1/2 yard bright blue solid for the inner border
- 3 5/8 yards light blue print
- 2 5/8 yards blue and pink print for the outer border and binding
- 5 yards backing fabric
- 80" x 95" piece of batting

Cutting
Dimensions include a 1/4" seam allowance. Cut lengthwise strips before cutting other pieces from the same yardage.
- Cut 98: 3" squares, pink print
- Cut 198: 3" squares, assorted blue prints
- Cut 49: 3" squares, turquoise print
- Cut 196: 3" squares, light blue print
- Cut 50: 8" squares, light blue print
- Cut 8: 1 1/2" x 44" strips, bright blue solid, for the inner border
- Cut 4: 2 1/2" x 90" lengthwise strips, blue and pink print, for the binding
- Cut 2: 3 1/2" x 87" lengthwise strips, blue and pink print, for the outer border
- Cut 2: 3 1/2" x 78" lengthwise strips, blue and pink print, for the outer border

Directions

For the modified Snowball blocks:
1. Referring to the *General Directions* for Snowball construction, stitch a modified Snowball block using an 8" light blue print square and two 3" assorted blue print squares for opposite Snowball corners, as shown. Make 50.

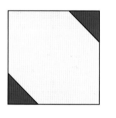

For the Nine Patch blocks:
1. Lay out two 3" pink print squares, four 3" light blue squares, one 3" turquoise print square, and two 3" assorted blue print squares in 3 rows of 3, as shown.

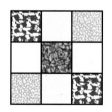

2. Stitch the squares into rows and join the rows to make a Nine Patch block. Make 49.

Assembly
1. Referring to the quilt photo, lay out the modified Snowball blocks alternately with the Nine Patch blocks in 11 rows of 9.
2. Stitch the blocks into rows and join the rows.
3. Stitch two 1 1/2" x 44" bright blue solid strips together, end to end, to make an inner border. Make 4.
4. Measure the length of the quilt. Trim 2 inner borders to that measurement and stitch them to the long sides of the quilt.
5. Measure the width of the quilt, including the borders. Trim the remaining inner borders to that measurement and stitch them to the remaining sides of the quilt.
6. In the same manner, trim two 3 1/2" x 87" blue and pink print strips to fit the quilt's length and stitch them to the sides of the quilt.
7. Trim the 3 1/2" x 78" blue and pink print strips to fit the quilts width and stitch them to the quilt.
8. Finish the quilt as described in the *General Directions,* using the 2 1/2" x 90" blue and pink print strips for the binding.

Nine Patch and Snowball Scrap Quilt

Rose Warner and her daughter Rosella Hennessey of Inglis, Florida, made many quilts together each year before Rose passed away at the age of 99. Rose would sometimes stitch blocks by machine, but most of the time, she did the hand quilting. Their collaboration yielded this simple, yet elegant **"Nine Patch and Snowball Scrap Quilt".**

Quilt Size: 90" x 102"
Block Size: 6" square

Materials

- Assorted blue prints, totaling 4 yards
- Assorted light, medium, and dark prints, totaling 4 1/2 yards
- 3 1/2 yards white-on-white print
- 3 yards navy blue print for the borders and binding
- 8 yards backing fabric
- 94" x 106" piece of batting

Cutting

All dimensions include a 1/4" seam allowance. Cut the lengthwise strips before cutting other pieces from the same yardage.

- Cut 448: 2 1/2" squares, assorted blue prints, for the Snowball blocks
- Cut 1008: 2 1/2" squares, assorted light, medium, and dark prints, for the Nine Patch blocks
- Cut 112: 6 1/2" squares, white-on-white print
- Cut 4: 3 1/2" x 100" lengthwise strips, navy blue print, for the borders
- Cut 4: 2 1/2" x 108" lengthwise strips, navy blue print, for the binding

Directions

For the Snowball blocks:

1. Referring to the *General Directions* for Snowball construction, stitch a Snowball block using one 6 1/2" white-on-white print square and four 2 1/2" blue print squares, as shown. Make 112. Set them aside.

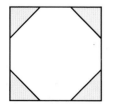

For the Nine Patch blocks:

1. Referring to the *General Directions* for Nine Patch blocks, Method #2, stitch Nine Patch blocks using 2 1/2" assorted light, medium, and dark print squares, as shown. Make 112.

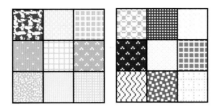

Assembly

1. Lay out the Snowball and Nine Patch blocks alternately in 16 rows of 14. Stitch the blocks into rows and join the rows.

2. Measure the length of the quilt. Trim 2 of the 3 1/2" x 100" navy blue strips to that measurement and stitch them to the long sides of the quilt.

3. Measure the width of the quilt, including the borders. Trim the remaining 3 1/2" x 100" navy blue print strips to that measurement and stitch them to the remaining sides of the quilt.

4. Finish the quilt as described in the *General Directions,* using the 2 1/2" x 108" navy blue print strips for the binding.

Quilting Design for Nine Patch and Snowball Scrap

Apple Blossom Time

*Stitching Nine Patch and Snowball blocks in groups of four before combining them into a quilt provides a new twist on this old favorite. Rose Warner, Rosella Hennessey, and Louise Feldt, members of Miss Kitty's Quilter's Guild of Dodge City, Kansas, stitched the blocks at a quilting party I hosted. **"Apple Blossom Time"** was machine quilted by Shelly Carmichael of Larned, Kansas.*

Quilt Size: 74" x 98"
Block Size: 6" square

Materials
- 2 1/4 yards white-on-white print
- 3 1/2 yards dark blue print for the blocks, inner and outer borders and binding
- 1 1/2 yards light blue print
- 3/4 yard yellow print for the blocks and middle border
- 3/4 yard medium green print
- 3/4 yard dark green print
- 6 yards backing fabric
- 78" x 102" piece of batting

Cutting
Dimensions include a 1/4" seam allowance. Cut lengthwise pieces before cutting other pieces from the same yardage.
- Cut 68: 6 1/2" squares, white-on-white print
- Cut 4: 1" x 85" lengthwise strips, dark blue print, for the inner border
- Cut 4: 6 1/2" x 87" lengthwise strips, dark blue print, for the outer border
- Cut 4: 2 1/2" x 96" lengthwise strips, dark blue print, for the binding
- Cut 204: 2 1/2" squares, dark blue print
- Cut 10: 2 1/2" x 44" strips, dark blue print
- Cut 8: 1" x 44" strips, yellow print, for the middle border
- Cut 68: 2 1/2" squares, yellow print
- Cut 8: 2 1/2" x 44" strips, medium green print
- Cut 8: 2 1/2" x 44" strips, dark green print
- Cut 22: 2 1/2" x 44" strips, light blue print

Directions
For the Apple Blossom squares:
1. Referring to the *General Directions* for Snowball construction, stitch a Snowball block using a 6 1/2" white-on-white print square, three 2 1/2" dark blue print squares, and one 2 1/2" yellow print square, as shown. Make 68.

2. Lay out 4 Snowball blocks in 2 rows of 2, as shown. Stitch the blocks into pairs and join the pairs to make an Apple Blossom square. Make 17.

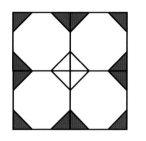

For the Nine Patch squares:
1. Referring to the *General Directions* for the Nine Patch blocks, Method #1, stitch a 2 1/2" x 44" light blue print strip between a 2 1/2" x 44" medium green print strip and a 2 1/2" x 44" dark blue print strip to make a pieced panel. Press the seam allowances toward the light blue. Make 5.

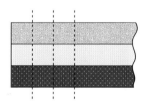

2. Cut seventy-two 2 1/2" slices from the pieced panels. Label them #1 and set them aside.
3. Stitch a 2 1/2" x 44" medium green print strip between two 2 1/2" x 44" light blue strips to make a pieced panel. Press the seam allowances toward the light blue print. Make 3.

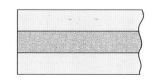

4. Cut thirty-six 2 1/2" slices from

them. Label them #2.
5. Stitch two #1 slices and one #2 slice together, as shown, to make a Nine Patch. Make 36. Label them "A" and set them aside.

6. Stitch a 2 1/2" x 44" light blue print strip between a 2 1/2" x 44" dark green print strip and a dark blue print strip. Make 5. Press the seam allowances toward the light blue print strip.
7. Cut seventy-two 2 1/2" slices from the pieced panels. Label them #3.
8. Stitch a 2 1/2" x 44" dark green print strip between two light blue print strips to make a pieced panel. Make 3. Press the seam allowances toward the light blue print.
9. Cut thirty-six 2 1/2" slices from the pieced panels. Label them #4.
10. Lay out two #3 slices and one #4 slice, as shown, to make a "B" Nine Patch. Make 36.

11. Lay out two "A" Nine Patches and two "B" Nine Patches in 2 rows of 2. Stitch the blocks into pairs and join the pairs to make a Nine Patch square. Make 18.

(Continued on page 28)

Twisted Ribbons

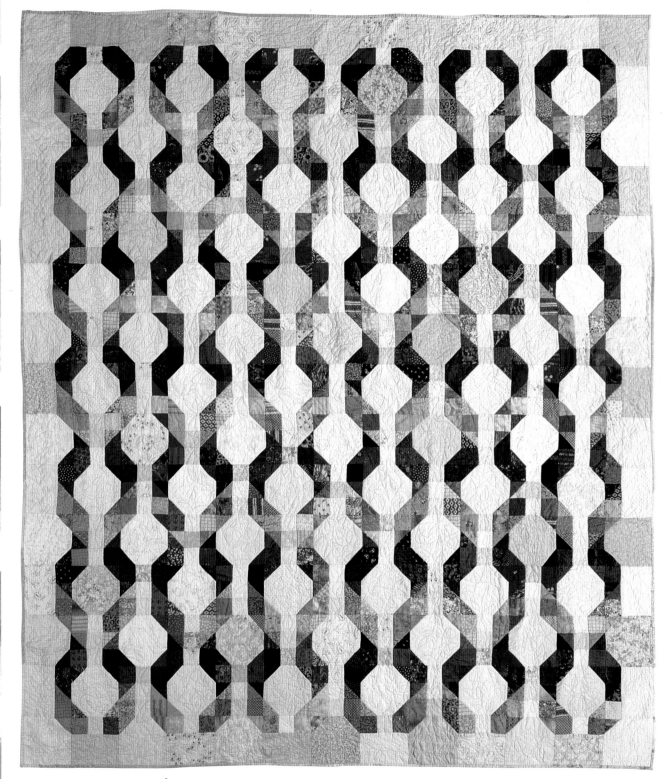

Value and color play an important role in creating the impression of spiraled ribbons like those on an unopened birthday present. **"Twisted Ribbons"** *was such fun to plan and make. I loved playing with my fabric scraps, and these wonderful colors! When making your version, don't get too concerned about matching value and color in the prints or you'll lose some of the wonderful vitality of working scrappy.*

Quilt Size: 78" x 90"
Block Size: 6" square

Materials

- Assorted light prints in 12 color families to total 3 yards
- Assorted dark prints in the same 12 color families to total 3 yards
- Assorted off-white prints to total 7 1/2 yards, for the blocks, border, and binding
- 5 3/8 yards backing fabric
- 82" x 94" piece of batting

Cutting

Dimensions include 1/4" seam allowance.

For the Snowball blocks and Snowball Edge and Corner units:

- Cut 98: 6 1/2" squares off-white prints
- Cut 14: 2 1/2" squares from each color of assorted light and dark print; then stack them in order by color group and label them #1 through #12

For the Nine Patch blocks and Nine Patch Edge units:

- Cut 14: 2 1/2" squares from each family of assorted light and coordinating dark prints; then stack them by color group and label them #1 through #12
- Cut 7: 2 7/8" squares from each family of assorted light and coordinating dark prints. Stack them by color group and label them #1 through #12.
- Cut 225: 2 1/2" squares, assorted off-white prints
- Cut 26: 4 1/2" x 6 1/2" rectangles, off-white prints

Also:

- Cut 20: 2 1/2" x 22" strips, assorted off-white prints, for the binding

Directions

For the Snowball blocks:

1. Referring to the *General Directions* for Snowball construction, stitch a Snowball block using a 6 1/2" off-white print square, one 2 1/2" square each of #1 and #2 light prints and one 2 1/2" square each of #1 and #2 coordinating dark prints, as shown. Make 7. Label them column 1. NOTE: *Keep the light prints on the bottom of the blocks and the dark prints on the top. Be sure to keep the numbered squares in order from left to right. Refer to the Assembly Diagram on page 27.*

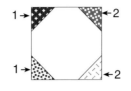

2. In the same manner, make 7 Snowball blocks each of the following color combinations and set them aside:

    #3 and #4, label them column 3
    #5 and #6, label them column 5
    #7 and #8, label them column 7
    #9 and #10, label them column 9
    #11 and #12, label them column 11

3. Lay out one 6 1/2" off-white print square, one 2 1/2" square each of #2 and #3 light prints and one 2 1/2" square each of #2 and #3 coordinating dark prints. Stitch them into a Snowball block, as shown. Make 6. Label them column 2. NOTE: *Keep the dark prints on the bottom of the blocks and the light prints on the top.*

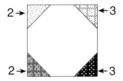

4. In the same manner, make 6 Snowball blocks each of the following color combinations and set them aside:

    #4 and #5, label them column 4
    #6 and #7, label them column 6
    #8 and #9, label them column 8
    #10 and #11, label them column 10

For the Snowball Edge and Corner units:

1. Lay out a 6 1/2" off-white print square and one each of #1 light and coordinating prints placing the light square in the top position. Stitch them into a Snowball Edge unit, as shown. Make 6. Label them Left Edge Snowball units and set them aside.

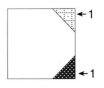

2. In the same manner make 6 Right Edge Snowball units, using #12 light and dark coordinating prints, as shown. Label them and set them aside.

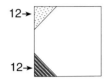

3. Stitch 5 Top Edge Snowball units, as shown, using 6 1/2" off-white print squares and the following combinations of dark coordinating prints:

    #2 and #3 (column 2)
    #4 and #5 (column 4)
    #6 and #7 (column 6)
    #8 and #9 (column 8)
    #10 and #11 (column 10)

Label them and set them aside.

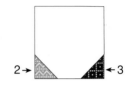

4. Stitch 5 Bottom Edge Snowball units, as shown, using 6 1/2" off-white print squares and the following combinations of light prints:

    #2 and #3 (column 2)
    #4 and #5 (column 4)
    #6 and #7 (column 6)
    #8 and #9 (column 8)
    #10 and #11 (column 10)

Label them and set them aside.

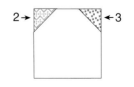

5. Stitch a Corner unit, as shown, using a 6 1/2" off-white print square and one 2 1/2" #1 light print square.

(Continued on page 26)

Lazy Daisies

Who says all Snowballs have to be white? Not me! Stitching the Snowballs from dark prints and reversing the values in the Nine Patch blocks creates a chain effect around the Snowballs. Turning the blocks on point further interrupts your perception of square blocks, making **"Lazy Daisies"** *appear to be much more complicated to make than it actually is. Make the matching pillow shams and dresser scarf for a complete bedroom makeover!*

Quilt Size: 82" x 92"
Block Size: 6" square

Materials

- Assorted medium to dark prints, at least 10" square, to total 5 yards
- 3/4 yard gold solid
- 6 yards muslin
- 1/8 yard white-on-white print for the flowers (A)
- 1/8 yard green solid for the stems and leaves (C & D)
- 6" square of ecru batik for the butterfly (E)
- 6" square of orange batik for the butterfly (F, G, and H)
- 5 1/2 yards backing fabric
- Fusible web
- 86" x 96" piece of batting

Cutting

Patterns (page 26) for fusible appliqué are full size and do not need a turn-under allowance. Trace each pattern on the paper side of the fusible web. Cut out the shapes slightly beyond the drawn lines. Following the manufacturer's directions, fuse the shapes to the wrong side of the appropriate fabrics. Cut the fabric shapes out on the drawn lines. All other dimensions include a 1/4" seam allowance. Cut the lengthwise strips before cutting other pieces from the same yardage.

- Cut 63: 6 1/2" squares, assorted medium to dark prints
- Cut 320: 2 1/2" squares, assorted medium to dark prints
- Cut 80: 2 1/2" squares, gold solid
- Cut 6: 1 1/2" x 44" strips, gold solid, for the inner border
- Cut 572: 2 1/2" squares, muslin
- Cut 8: 10" squares muslin, then cut them in quarters diagonally to yield 32 setting triangles
- Cut 2: 5 1/2" squares, muslin, then cut them in half diagonally to yield 4 corner triangles
- Cut 3: 6 1/2" x 90" lengthwise strips, muslin, for the outer border
- Cut 4: 2 1/2" x 96" lengthwise strips, muslin, for the binding

For the appliqués:

- Cut 5: flowers, white-on-white print
- Cut 5: flower centers, gold solid
- Cut 5: stems, green solid
- Cut 5: leaves, green solid
- Cut 1: butterfly, ecru batik
- Cut 1 each: A and AR, orange batik
- Cut 1 each: B and BR, orange batik
- Cut 1 each: C and CR, orange batik

Directions

For the Snowball blocks:

1. Referring to the *General Directions* for Snowball construction, stitch a Snowball block, using one 6 1/2" medium to dark print square and four 2 1/2" muslin squares, as shown. Make 63. Set them aside.

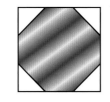

For the Nine Patch blocks:

1. Referring to the *General Directions* for Nine Patch blocks, Method #2, stitch a Nine Patch block, using four 2 1/2" assorted medium to dark print squares, one 2 1/2" gold solid square, and four 2 1/2" muslin squares, as shown. Make 80.

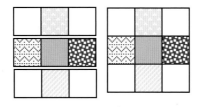

Assembly

1. Referring to the quilt photo for placement, lay out the Snowball blocks, Nine Patch blocks, and setting and corner triangles in diagonal rows. Stitch the blocks into rows and join the rows.

2. If needed, trim to straighten the edges of the quilt.

3. Stitch two 1 1/2" x 44" gold solid strips together, end to end to make an inner border. Make 3.

4. Measure the length of the quilt. Trim 2 of the inner borders to that measurement and stitch them to the long sides of the quilt.

5. Measure the width of the quilt, including the borders. Trim the remaining inner border to that measurement and stitch it to the bottom of the quilt. NOTE: *There is only one top border. The matching pillow shams will cover the top of the quilt when it is on a bed.*

6. In the same manner, trim two of the 6 1/2" x 90" muslin strips to fit the length of the quilt. Stitch them to the long sides of the quilt.

7. Trim the remaining 6 1/2" x 90" muslin strip to fit the width of the quilt and stitch it to the bottom of the quilt.

8. Remove the paper backing from the flower and butterfly appliqué shapes. Referring to the quilt photo, place the shapes on 6 Snowball blocks and fuse them in place. Blanket or satin stitch around the appliqué edges, if desired.

9. Finish the quilt according to the *General Directions*, using the 2 1/2" x 96" muslin strips for the binding.

Note: The quilting motifs that were used on this quilt are on the inside back cover.

Lazy Daisies Dresser Scarf & Pillow Shams

Make the **"Lazy Daisies Dresser Scarf"** to match your quilt and pillow shams. Remember, you can change the colors, fabrics, and appliqués to match your quilt. It doesn't have to be made in the "Lazy Daisy" pattern! Wouldn't holiday guests be delighted if these coordinates were made in Christmas colors and prints, or how about country colors to match a country decorating theme? The possibilities are endless.

The Snowball blocks in **"Lazy Daisies Pillow Shams"** showcase one of my favorite large prints of cats in a garden of daisies and other flowers. Although these pillow shams are designed to coordinate with my quilt "Lazy Daisies" you could make them to go with any of the bed quilts given in this book. How about adding heart appliqués to the Snowballs for "Hearts of Gold," or stars for "Country Stars"? The choice is yours.

Dresser Scarf Size: 20" x 55"
Block Size: 6" square

Materials

- Assorted medium to dark prints to total 3/4 yard
- Fat eighth (11" x 18") gold solid
- 1 yard muslin
- 1 2/3 yards of backing fabric
- 24" x 60" piece of batting

Cutting

Patterns for fusible appliqué are full size and do not need a turn-under allowance. Trace each pattern on the paper side of the fusible web. Cut out the shapes slightly beyond the drawn lines. Following the manufacturer's directions, fuse the shapes to the wrong side of the appropriate fabrics. Cut the fabric shapes out on the drawn lines. All other dimensions include a 1/4" seam allowance. Cut the lengthwise strips before cutting other pieces from the same yardage.

- Cut 6: 6 1/2" squares assorted medium to dark prints
- Cut 40: 2 1/2" squares assorted medium to dark prints
- Cut 10: 2 1/2" squares gold solid
- Cut 64: 2 1/2" squares muslin
- Cut 2: 13 1/2" squares muslin, then cut them in quarters diagonally to yield 8 large triangles NOTE: *These triangles are larger than needed to provide a 1 1/2" border outside the blocks.*
- Cut 4: 2 1/2" x 16" strips muslin
- Cut 5: 2 1/2" x 44" strips muslin, for the binding

Also:

- Cut 2: flowers, white-on-white print
- Cut 2: flower centers, gold solid
- Cut 2: stems, green solid
- Cut 2: leaves, green solid

Directions

For the Snowball blocks:

1. Referring to the *General Directions* for Snowball construction, stitch a Snowball block, using one 6 1/2" medium to dark print square and four 2 1/2" muslin squares, as shown. Make 6. Set them aside.

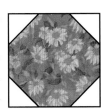

For the Nine Patch blocks:

1. Referring to the *General Directions* for Nine Patch blocks, Method #2, stitch a Nine Patch block, using four 2 1/2" assorted medium to dark print squares, one 2 1/2" gold solid square, and four 2 1/2" muslin squares, as shown. Make 10.

Assembly

1. Lay out 6 Snowball blocks, 10 Nine Patch blocks, and 8 triangles in diagonal rows, as shown. NOTE: *The triangles will extend beyond the edges of the Nine Patch blocks.*

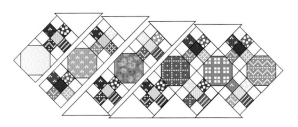

2. Stitch the blocks and triangles into rows and join the rows. Trim the extra fabric from behind the triangle edges, leaving a 1/4" seam allowance.

3. Trim the triangles 1 3/4" beyond the points of the Nine Patch blocks.

4. Stitch 2 1/2" x 16" muslin strips to 2 opposite corners of the dresser scarf, and trim the ends as shown.

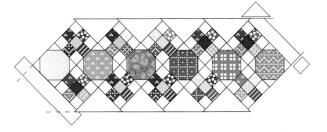

5. Stitch 2 1/2" x 16" muslin strips to the remaining corners, and trim the outer edges even, as shown.

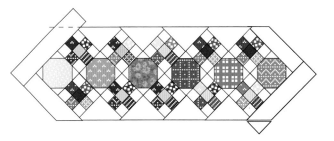

6. Remove the paper backing from the flower appliqué shapes. Referring to the photo, fuse the appliqués to the Snowball blocks at opposite ends of the Dresser Scarf. Blanket or satin stitch around the appliqué edges, if desired.

7. Finish the Dresser Scarf according to the *General Directions*, using the 2 1/2" x 44" muslin strips for the binding.

Pillow Sham Size: 19 1/2" x 27 1/2"
Block Size: 6" square

Materials

- Assorted medium to dark prints to total 5/8 yard (I chose a coordinating cat novelty print for the Snowball blocks.)
- Fat eighth (11" x 18") gold solid
- 4 1/4 yards muslin
- Two 22" x 30" pieces of batting

Cutting

All dimensions include a 1/4" seam allowance.

- Cut 6: 6 1/2" squares, assorted medium to dark prints
- Cut 64: 2 1/2" squares, assorted medium to dark prints
- Cut 16: 2 1/2" squares, gold solid
- Cut 4: 20" x 24" rectangles, muslin, for the pillow sham backs
- Cut 2: 22" x 30" rectangles, muslin
- Cut 6: 5" x 60" strips, muslin, for the ruffles
- Cut 3: 13 1/2" squares muslin, then cut them in quarters diagonally, to yield 12 large triangles *NOTE: These triangles are larger than needed to provide a 1 1/2" border outside the blocks.*
- Cut 6: 8 1/2" squares muslin, then cut them in half diagonally, to yield 12 small triangles
- Cut 88: 2 1/2" squares, muslin

Directions

For the Snowball blocks:

1. Referring to the *General Directions* for Snowball construction, stitch a Snowball block, using four 2 1/2" muslin squares and one 6 1/2" medium to dark or cat novelty print square, as shown. Make 6. Set them aside.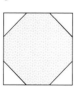

For the Nine Patch blocks:

1. Referring to the *General Directions* for Nine Patch blocks, Method #2, stitch a Nine Patch block, using four 2

1/2" assorted medium to dark print squares, one 2 1/2" gold solid square, and four 2 1/2" muslin squares, as shown. Make 16.

Assembly for each of 2 Pillow Shams

1. Lay out 3 Snowball blocks, 8 Nine Patch blocks, and 6 large and 6 small triangles in diagonal rows, as shown.

2. Stitch the blocks and triangles into rows and join the rows to make a pillow top.

3. Trim the pillow top to 20" x 28", trimming an equal amount from each end to keep the Snowball blocks centered.

4. Layer the pillow top, a 22" x 30" piece of batting, and a 22" x 30" rectangle of muslin. Baste the layers and quilt as desired. Set it aside.

5. Stitch three 5" x 60" muslin strips together, end to end. Stitch the remaining ends together to make a loop.

6. Press the loop in half lengthwise, right side out and matching the raw edges, as shown.

7. To gather the ruffle, set your machine to a long stitch length (4 to 6 stitches per inch) and stitch 1/8" and 3/8" from the raw edges of the loop.

8. Divide the ruffle in quarters by folding it in half and then in half again. Mark the folds with a pin.

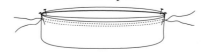

9. Pin the ruffle to the pillow top, matching the quarter marks with the center of the sides of the pillow top. Gather by pulling the bobbin threads of the large stitches. Round the corners slightly, and move more gathers toward the corners than on the sides.

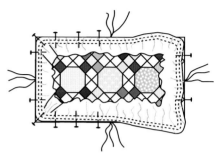

10. Baste the ruffle to the right side of the pillow top between the lines of gathering stitches.

11. Turn under 1/4" along one 20"-long edge of each of two 20" x 24" muslin rectangles. Stitch to make a hemmed edge.

12. Press under 4" of the hemmed edge. Hold the hemmed edge in place by basting along the outer edges.

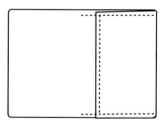

13. Lay the prepared muslin rectangles on the pillow top and ruffle, right sides together and overlapping the hemmed edges. Pin.

14. With the wrong side of the pillow top facing up, stitch around the edges, stitching exactly on the ruffle basting stitches.

15. Turn the pillow top right sides out through the opening in the pillow back.

16. Insert a full-sized bed pillow.

Quilting Design for
Lazy Daisies (Page 20)

Appliqué Patterns for
Lazy Daisies (Page 20)

B

A

C

Flower Pattern also used as
Quilting Design for Snowball Blocks

(continued from page 19)

Make a second Corner unit using a 2 1/2" #12 light print square.

6. In the same manner, make 2 Corner units using 6 1/2" off-white print squares and 2 1/2" #1 and #12 dark coordinating print squares.

For the Nine Patch blocks:

NOTE: *You will be working with 2 color groups at a time. Begin with #1 and #2, then work your way through the colors.*

1. Draw a diagonal line from corner to corner on the wrong side of a 2 7/8" #1 light print square.

2. Lay a marked square on a 2 7/8" coordinating dark print square, right sides together, and stitch 1/4" away from the drawn line on both sides, as shown. Make 7.

3. Cut on the drawn lines to yield 14 pieced squares. Press the seam allowance toward the dark print.

4. In the same manner, make 14 pieced squares from each of the light and coordinating dark print color groups. Set them aside.

5. Lay out three 2 1/2" assorted off-white print squares, one each of the #1 and #2 pieced squares, and one each of #1 and #2 light print squares and coordinating dark print squares in 3 rows of 3, as shown. Stitch them into a Nine Patch block. Make 6. Label them Column 1 and set them aside.

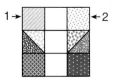

6. In the same manner, make 6 Nine Patch blocks from each of the following color combinations:

   #3 and #4 (Column 3)
   #5 and #6 (Column 5
   #7 and #8 (Column 7)
   #9 and #10 (Column 9)
   #11 and #12 (Column 11)

7. Lay out three 2 1/2" assorted off-white print squares, one each of the #2 and #3 pieced squares, and one each of #2 and #3 light and coordinating dark print squares in 3 rows of 3. Stitch them into a Nine Patch block, as shown. Make 7. Label them Column 2 and set them aside.

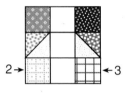

8. In the same manner, make 7 Nine Patch blocks from each of the following color combinations:

   #4 and #5 (Column 4)
   #6 and #7 (Column 6)
   #8 and #9 (Column 8)
   #10 and #11 (Column 10)

Set them aside.

For the Nine Patch Edge units:

1. Stitch Left Edge Nine Patch units, as shown, using 4 1/2" x 6 1/2" assorted off-white print rectangles, 2 1/2" #1 bright and dark coordinating print squares and #1 pieced squares. Make 7.

2. Stitch Right Edge Nine Patch units, as shown, using 4 1/2" x 6 1/2" assorted off-white print rectangles, #12 light and dark coordinating prints squares and #12 pieced squares. Make 7.

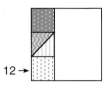

3. Stitch Top Edge Nine Patch units, as shown, using 4 1/2" x 6 1/2" assorted off-white print rectangles, off-white print squares, and dark coordinating print squares in color combinations for columns 1, 3, 5, 7, 9, and 11.

4. Stitch Bottom Edge Nine Patch units, as shown, using 4 1/2" x 6 1/2" assorted off-white print rectangles, off-white print squares, and bright print squares in color combinations for columns 1, 3, 5, 7, 9, and 11.

Assembly

1. Referring to the quilt photo, lay out the units in 13 vertical rows in this order: Left Edge units, columns 1 through 11, and Right Edge units. Lay out the top row with Corner and Top units and the bottom row with Corner and Bottom units. Pay careful attention to orientation of the blocks, so that they form a twisted ribbon pattern.

2. Stitch the blocks into vertical rows, and join the rows.

3. Finish the quilt as described in the *General Directions,* using the 2 1/2" x 22" assorted off-white print strips for the binding.

Assembly Diagram for Twisted Ribbons

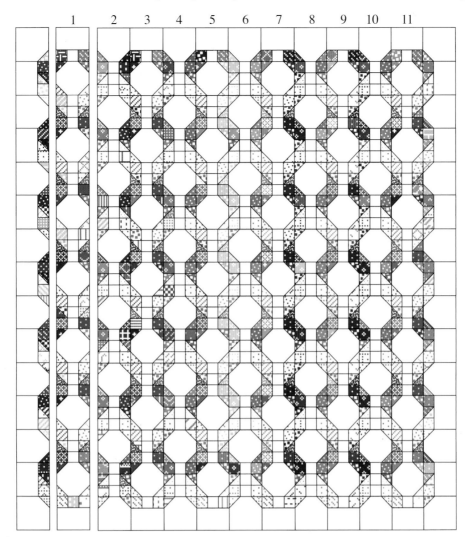

1 2 3 4 5 6 7 8 9 10 11

Hearts of Gold

(continued from page 5)

ment and stitch them to the top and bottom of the quilt.

4. Stitch two 3/4" x 44" gold print strips together, end to end, to make a border. Make 4.

5. Trim 2 of the gold borders to fit the length of the quilt and stitch them to the sides of the quilt.

6. Trim the remaining gold borders to fit the width of the quilt and stitch them to the top and bottom of the quilt.

7. In the same manner, trim the 5 1/2" x 70" dark blue print strips to fit the quilt's length and stitch them to the quilt.

8. Trim the 5 1/2" x 56" dark blue print strips to fit the quilt's width and stitch them to the top and bottom of the quilt.

9. Finish the quilt as described in the *General Directions*, using the 2 1/2" x 72" dark blue print strips for the binding.

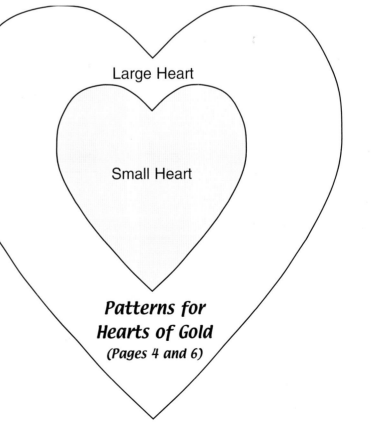

Large Heart

Small Heart

Patterns for Hearts of Gold
(Pages 4 and 6)

Internet

(continued from page 11)

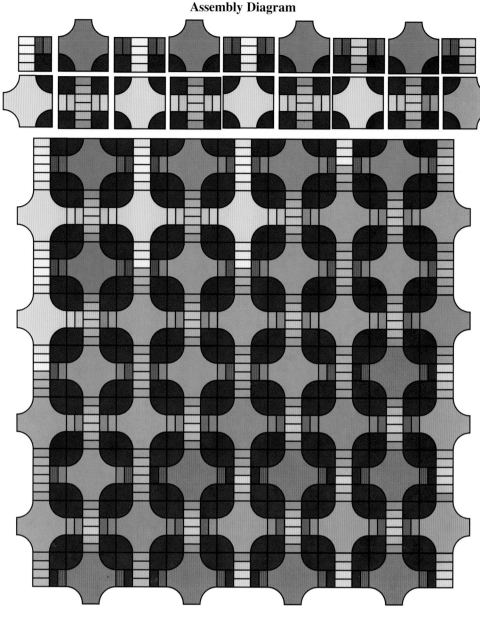

Assembly

1. Referring to the Assembly Diagram, lay out the corners and partial and full Nine Patch and Snowball blocks in 11 rows of 9. Be sure to place the Nine Patch blocks with the light bands of color running vertically.

2. Stitch the blocks into rows and join the rows.

3. Trim the partial Snowball blocks even with the edges of the partial Nine Patches.

4. Measure the length of the quilt. Trim two 3 1/2" x 68" black solid strips to that measurement and stitch them to the long sides of the quilt.

5. Measure the width of the quilt, including the borders. Trim the remaining 3 1/2" x 68" black solid strips to that measurement and stitch them to the remaining sides of the quilt.

6. Finish the quilt as described in the *General Directions,* using the 2 1/2" x 72" black solid strips for the binding.

Apple Blossom

(continued from page 17)

Assembly

1. Referring to the quilt photo (page 16), lay out the Apple Blossom squares alternately with the Nine Patch squares in 7 rows of 5. NOTE: *The dark green squares of the Nine Patch blocks form diagonal rows in one direction. The medium green squares form diagonal rows in the opposite direction.*

2. Stitch the squares into rows and join the rows.

3. Measure the length of the quilt. Trim two 1" x 85" dark blue print strips to that measurement and stitch them to the long sides of the quilt.

4. Measure the width of the quilt including the borders. Trim the remaining 1" x 85" dark blue print strips to that measurement and stitch them to the remaining sides of the quilt.

5. Stitch two 1" x 44" yellow print strips together, end to end, to make a middle border. Make 4.

6. Measure the length of the quilt. Trim 2 middle borders to that measurement and stitch them to the long sides of the quilt.

7. Measure the width of the quilt, including the borders. Trim the remaining middle borders to that measurement and stitch them to the remaining sides of the quilt.

8. In the same manner, trim two 6 1/2" x 87" dark blue print strips to fit the quilt's length and stitch them to the long sides of the quilt.

9. Trim the remaining 6 1/2" x 87" dark blue print strips to fit the remaining sides and stitch them to the quilt.

10. Finish the quilt as described in the *General Directions,* using the 2 1/2" x 96" dark blue print strips for the binding.

Pattern pieces for
Internet (Page 11)

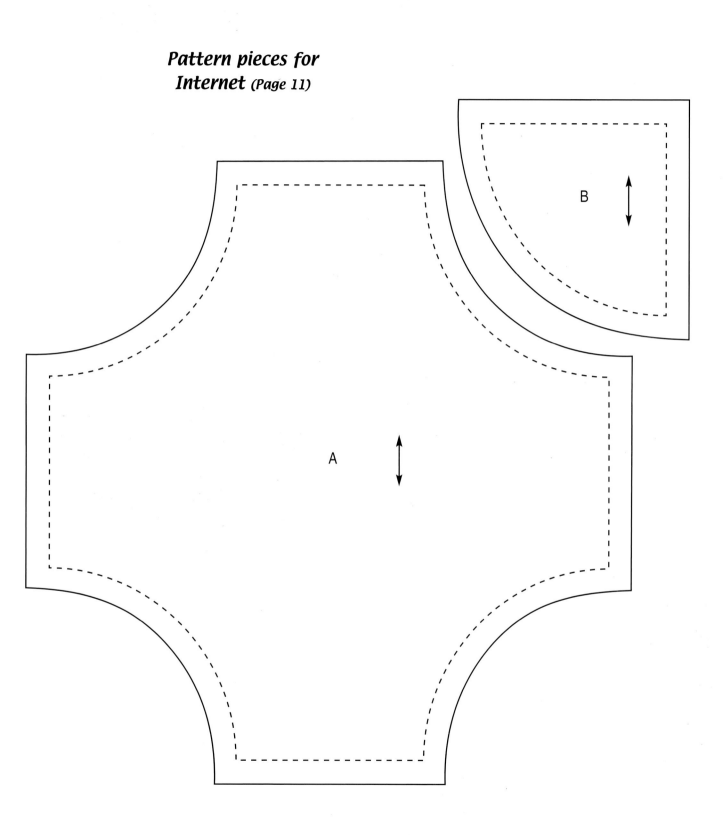

A

B

Country Stars

(continued from page 9)

lines so the finished unit will look like the diagram.

4. In the same manner, make Border units from the remaining 2 1/2" x 6 1/2" assorted white and off-white print strips and 2 1/2" light red print squares, as shown. Make 10. Set them aside.

5. Stitch a 2 1/2" red print square to one end of a 2 1/2" x 4 1/2" white or off-white print rectangle, as shown. Make 20. Set them aside.

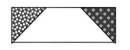

Assembly

1. Referring to the Assembly Diagram, lay out the Snowball and Nine Patch blocks, Border units, and 2 1/2" assorted white and off-white print corner squares in rows.

2. Stitch the blocks, Border units and corner squares into rows and join the rows.

3. Stitch two 2" x 44" tone-on-tone off-white print strips together end to end, to make an inner border. Make 4.

4. Measure the length of the quilt. Trim 2 inner borders to that measurement. Stitch them to the long sides of the quilt.

5. Measure the width of the quilt, including the borders. Trim the remaining inner borders to that measurement. Stitch them to the remaining sides of the quilt.

6. Stitch two 1 1/4" x 44" dark red print strips together end to end to make a middle border. Make 4.

7. In the same manner as for the inner borders, measure the quilt, trim the middle borders, and stitch them to the quilt.

8. Trim two 4 1/4" x 88" dark blue print strips to fit the quilt's length and stitch them to the long sides of the quilt.

9. Trim the remaining 4 1/4" x 88" dark blue print strips to fit the quilt's width and stitch them to the remaining sides of the quilt.

10. Finish the quilt as described in the *General Directions*, using the 2 1/2" x 96" dark blue print strips for the binding.

Note: The star quilting motifs that were used on this quilt are on the inside back cover.

Assembly Diagram

General Directions

Most of the projects in this book use 6" finished blocks. The strips or squares for the Nine Patches are cut 2 1/2" wide and the large squares for the Snowballs are cut 6 1/2" square. However, if you'd prefer a larger or smaller quilt than the one shown, you may do one of two things. You can choose to make more blocks. With this option, you'll need to make enough blocks to add another row or column or both to your quilt.

Your second option is to cut larger or smaller squares and strips. For a larger quilt, cut the strips or squares for the Nine Patches and Snowball corners 3" wide and cut the squares for the Snowballs 8" square. These blocks will finish at 7 1/2" square. The resulting quilt stitched from them will be 25% larger. Remember to buy at least 25% more fabric when enlarging the size.

For a smaller quilt, reduce the strip or square size to 2" for the Nine Patches and Snowball corners and 5" for the Snowballs. The finished block size will be 4 1/2" square and the quilt will be 25% smaller. I would not recommend reducing the yardage much when making this smaller size. I would rather have a little fabric left over than run out in the middle of a project.

About the Patterns

Read through the pattern directions before cutting fabric for the project. Pattern directions are given in step-by-step order. Pattern pieces for fusible web appliqué are full size and do not include a turn-under allowance. All other dimensions include a 1/4" seam allowance.

Fabric

I recommend using 100% cotton fabrics. Test all of your fabrics to be sure they are colorfast. I suggest washing your fabrics before using them. Yardage is based on 44" fabric with a useable width of 42".

Fusible Web

For larger appliqués, especially if they will have other appliqués fused on top of them, I trim the center from the cut fusible web piece before adhering it to the fabric. This reduces bulk and stiffness in the finished quilt. Trace the shape on the fusible web. Cut it out about 1/8" to 1/4" outside the line. Then cut 1/4" away from the line on the inside. Either discard the center or use it

for another appliqué piece.

Fuse the trimmed outline to the fabric and cut the piece out on the line. Fuse the piece to the desired fabric according to the manufacturer's directions.

Marking Fabric

Test all marking tools for removability before using them. I suggest using silver or white marking tools for dark fabrics and fine line pencils for light fabrics. Always use a sharp pencil and a light touch. Lay a piece of fine-grained sandpaper under the fabric to keep it from slipping while you mark it, if desired.

Machine Sewing

To make a stitching guide: Cut a length of masking tape or moleskin foot pad about 1/4" x 2". Place a clear plastic ruler under the presser foot to the left of the needle. Slowly slide the ruler to the right until the needle is aligned with the 1/4" mark on the ruler. Lower the presser foot to hold the ruler in place. Carefully adhere the moleskin on the throat plate along the right edge of the ruler. Feed fabric under the needle, touching this guide.

Set the stitch length to 12 stitches per inch. Stitch pieces together, from edge to edge unless directed to do otherwise in the pattern.

Nine Patch blocks:

Basic construction methods for Nine Patch blocks usually fall into two categories. I recommend the first method when all the Nine Patch blocks are identical. The second method is best for scrappy Nine Patch blocks. Refer to these instructions as needed when making your project.

Method #1:

Stitch strips into two panels in the order given in the pattern directions. For traditional Nine Patch blocks, this is usually light-dark-light, and dark-light-dark configuration. Press the seams toward the dark fabric. Cut 2 slices from the first panel and one slice from the second, and stitch them together to form a checkerboard pattern.

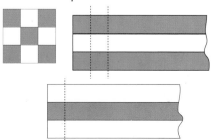

Method #2:

For a scrappy look, cut squares the size given in the pattern instructions. Sort them into light and dark values, and stitch them together into three rows of three. Join the rows to make a Nine Patch block.

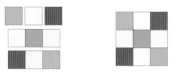

Snowball blocks:

The large open area of the Snowball blocks provides a great place to showcase novelty print fabrics. I like to position a selected motif in the center of the block. (See the Lazy Daisies pillow shams on page 22. I chose a large print with cat faces on it for the Snowball blocks.) It is also a great place to appliqué butterflies, flowers, or other favorite things. Or show off your hand quilting skills by quilting fancy feather designs in Snowballs made from solid-colored fabrics. The choice is yours.

Traditionally, Snowball blocks are made from a light value print or solid for the large part of the block. Dark triangles are stitched to each corner. However, some of the most interesting patterns reverse this value scheme, stitching light triangles in the corners of large, dark squares. Your pattern will provide cutting instructions for each project for the appropriate color scheme. The method I prefer for stitching traditional Snowball blocks begins with a large square and 4 small squares. Draw a diagonal line from corner to corner on the wrong side of each of the small squares. Then stitch a marked square to each corner of the large square, right sides together, aligning outer edges, and using the marked diagonal line as the stitching line. Open the small squares out, and press them toward the outside of the block, aligning the raw edges. Fold the corner back down, and trim the excess fabric 1/4" beyond the stitching line, as shown. Repeat for all four corners.

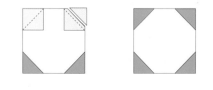

Pressing

Press seams toward the darker of the two

General Directions

fabrics unless otherwise noted. Press abutting seams in opposite directions whenever possible. Use a dry iron and press carefully, as little pieces are easy to distort.

FINISHING
Marking Quilting Designs

The quilting designs provided in this book fit a 6" Snowball block. You'll need to enlarge or reduce them if you choose to make larger or smaller blocks, or create your own motifs for your quilt. Use a special fabric from the quilt for inspiration.

I prefer to draft my quilting designs on a freezer paper square the same size as the block it will fit. First, I draw my design in pencil and fine tune it to suit me. Then I darken it with a Sharpie™ marker, iron it to the back of the quilt block, and trace it with my chosen fabric marking pen or pencil on the front of the block.

Simple designs can be cut from freezer paper or adhesive-backed shelf paper and adhered in position to the front of the quilt. Quilt around the design, remove it and reposition it on another part of the quilt. Avoid leaving any adhesive-backed paper on your quilt for longer than it takes to quilt the design. It may leave a sticky residue that is difficult to remove.

Mark lightly with pencils. Remember that what goes on must eventually come off! My favorite marking pencils are the Quilter's Ultimate Marking Pencil for light fabrics, and the Nonce™ white pencil for dark fabrics. Both are available at your favorite quilt shop. If not, ask for them. The shop owner can usually get them in a short time.

Batting

For hand quilting, I prefer a soft, easy-to-needle batting like a thin, bonded polyester or wool. For machine quilting, cotton is my preferred choice. It seems to 'grab' the cotton fabrics of the top and backing and hold the quilt sandwich together better as it travels under the needle.

Layer the quilt sandwich as follows: backing, wrong side up; batting; quilt top, right side up. Baste or pin the layers together. In addition, baste around the outer edges of the quilt about 3/16" away from the raw edge of the quilt top. These basting stitches will be covered with binding later, so they will not need to be removed.

Quilting

Small projects can be lap-quilted by hand without a hoop. When hand quilting, large projects are best quilted in a hoop or frame.

For hand quilting, use a short, thin needle (a "between" size 10 or higher) and small stitches. Thread the needle with a single strand of quilting thread and knot one end. Insert the needle through the quilt top and batting (not the backing) about 1/2" away from where you wish to begin the quilting line. Gently pull the thread to pop the knot through the top and bury it in the batting. Quilt as desired.

For machine quilting, use a fine, sharp needle (universal, denim, or quilting needle size 75/11 or 70/12) and a good quality cotton thread. If you choose to use invisible nylon thread, you may need to loosen the top tension on your machine. I prefer the YLI brand of .0004 monofilament for machine quilting.

Binding

Cut binding strips with the grain for straight-edge quilts. Binding for quilts with curved edges must be cut on the bias. To make 1/2" finished binding, cut 2 1/2"-wide strips. Sew strips together with diagonal seams; trim and press seam allowances open.

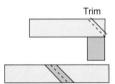

Fold the strip in half lengthwise, wrong side in, and press. Position the strip on the right side of the quilt top, aligning the raw edges of the binding with the edge of the quilt top. Leaving 6" of the binding strip free and beginning a few inches from one corner, stitch the binding to the quilt with a 1/4" seam allowance measuring from the raw edge of the quilt top. When you reach a corner, stop stitching 1/4" from the edge of the quilt top and backstitch. Clip the threads and remove the quilt from the machine. Fold the binding up and away from the quilt, forming a 45° angle, as shown.

Keeping the angled fold secure, fold the binding back down. This fold should be 1/4" beyond the edge of the quilt top. Begin stitching at the fold.

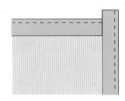

Continue stitching around the quilt in this manner to within 6" of the starting point. To finish, fold both strips back along the edge of the quilt so that the folded edges meet about 3" from both lines of stitching and the binding lies flat on the quilt. Finger press to crease the folds. Measure the width of the folded binding. Cut the strips that distance beyond the folds. (In this case 1 1/4" beyond the folds.)

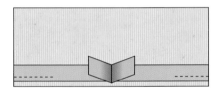

Open both strips and place the ends at right angles to each other, right sides together. Fold the bulk of the quilt out of your way. Join the strips with a diagonal seam as shown.

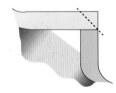

Trim the seam allowance to 1/4" and press it open. Refold the strip wrong side in. Place the binding flat against the quilt, and finish stitching it to the quilt. Trim excess batting and backing so that the binding edge will be filled with batting when you fold the binding to the back of the quilt. Blindstitch the binding to the back, covering the seamline.

Remove visible markings. Make a label that includes your name, the date the quilt was completed, and any other pertinent information, and stitch it to the back of your quilt. Sign and date your quilt.